HERBAL BIRTH CONTROL

D1713717

HYGEIA

Goddess of Pharmacy

HERBAL BIRTH CONTROL

A BRIEF HISTORY
WITH
ANCIENT AND MODERN
HERBAL RECIPES

by

R. R. McGREGOR

CLOUD CHIEF PUBLISHING
Weatherford, Oklahoma

Cloud Chief Publishing
PO Box 1664
Weatherford, OK 73096

Printed in the United States of America

ISBN 0-9636602-0-9

The plant illustrations in this volume are derived from Government or Federally-funded publications available in the U.S. Department of Agriculture Library, Beltsville, MD.

Front Cover Illustration: Author's rendition of the iconography of a Cyrenian four-drachma coin. The plant is Silphion (Ferula historica), a contraceptive plant which was the chief export of Cyrene, an Ancient Greek city-state. The plant's contraceptive property is indicated by the seated woman pointing to it with one hand, while her other hand points to her genital area. Attempts to grow the plant elsewhere failed, and it's popularity and apparent effectiveness led to its being harvested to extinction. After this, the Cyrenian economy declined rapidly.

To All the Daughters of Eve

CONTENTS

CONTENTS

Preface

The purpose of this small volume is to introduce the knowledge of some ancient herbal remedies to a general audience. The author is neither a physician nor an expert herbalist but a writer and researcher who believes that ordinary people can and must be trusted with knowledge in order to make rational judgements about their own health.

Gaining such knowledge is often difficult, especially when the subject is controlling human reproduction. Recent studies show that people have used plants to control fertility for over three thousand years but, for various reasons, this knowledge has almost died out. The continuous political and religious struggles over the legality of controlling reproduction, combined with the reluctance of Medical Doctors to recognize, much less endorse, the efficacy of many ancient remedies, has placed much reproductive knowledge on a par with classified Secret Service documents.

Women have died from overdoses of essential oils from plants which they apparently heard could cause abortions. It is hoped, by replacing rumors with facts, that this volume can help prevent such tragedies.

This volume gives certain recipes for herbal contraceptives and abortifacients, but in no way recommends their use. There are a great many variables involved in herbal remedies which make it difficult to determine dosage, and too strong a dose can be dangerous.

**The knowledge presented here
is for information only.
It is not qualified medical advice.**

A MEDIEVAL MIDWIFE AT WORK

INTRODUCTION

The Crime: *...when the woman saw that the tree was good for food, and that it was pleasant to the eyes, and a tree to be desired to make one wise; she took of the fruit thereof, and did eat; and gave also unto her husband with her, and he did eat.*
Genesis 3:6

The Punishment: *...Unto the woman he said, I will greatly multiply thy sorrow and thy conception; in sorrow thou shalt bring forth children: and thy desire shall be to thy husband, and he shall rule over thee.*
Genesis 3:16

It is said that there was once a time when women and men were equal in the eyes of the gods. Some even go so far as to say that human society was once matriarchal, that women made the laws and were revered above men as the creators of life. If this is so it was a very long time ago, before recorded history began.

From the prehistoric agricultural society of Sumer there is some evidence of an early reverence for woman. The earliest known creation myth says that the Sumerian goddess Nammu (the sea) gave birth unaided to the heavens and the earth, creating the universe. But this myth was rewritten many times by Sumer's conquerors, by many waves of male-dominated nomadic tribes who left the harsher life of tending animal herds in the highlands for the more placid existence in the lush valleys of the Fertile Crescent. All other creation myths since then involve male gods, up to and including the Hebrew god who is said to have made the universe with his Word alone, and female gods, like women, have held a secondary status ever since.

It is said that societies became male-dominated when men realized the part they played in human

1

reproduction. To a prelinguistic, prehistoric family group the relationship between sex and birth may not have been obvious, and for a woman to bring forth a child may have seemed magical and powerful, an indication that women deserved a special status. In time, however, men realized that women could not produce children alone, that they were powerless without the seed of the male.

It is possible that this discovery was made in agricultural societies, that a man one day saw the connection between planting a seed in the ground and then harvesting the grain, and realized the similarity to sex and birth. Some historians say, though, that the discovery would have been made sooner in the tribes of nomadic hunters who roamed the plains and highlands of central Asia. When instead of simply following herds, the tribes learned to manage them, they would have seen quite soon that herds of females would not bear young without males. They also would have seen that one male could fertilize an entire herd of females. This would have seemed powerful indeed, and it is no wonder that evidence indicates that, in nomadic tribes, women were held by men as chattel property, just like the herds, dogs, and other accoutrements of nomadic life.

We don't really know what happened four or five thousand years ago, of course. All this is simply edu-cated guesswork. But we do know that, regarding the status of women in society, the worldview of a dozen tribes of ragged desert nomads has, through a long series of wills, wars, and bizarre historical accidents, come to dominate all of western civilization. Such is the power of ideas when combined with the aggressive nature of testosterone.

Today, thanks to those who fought for freedom and caused the decline in the secular power of religion, women are gaining legal equality. Also, thanks to those who worked to develop relatively safe and predictable modern contraceptive methods, women are gaining the career opportunities and sexual freedoms so long enjoyed only by men. But women still do not have the absolute legal right to choose whether or not to carry a pregnancy to term, and the limited right they now have to end a pregnancy is in jeopardy.

For at least eight hundred years women were legally bound to their biological nature, able to avoid having children only by avoiding the pleasures of sex. This changed in this century with the development of effective birth control methods, but only after series of long, bitter legal struggles, and for more than a decade after The Pill women were still forced to continue pregnancies when "accidents" happened.

Also, because single women who use or plan for the use of birth control are too often viewed by men as "bad" or "loose" or "wanton", many women, in an effort to maintain the image of innocence and chastity desired by such men, don't adequately prepare for sexual encounters. Though it may seem anachronistic today, many men still hold a double standard. They want to have sex, but they want to marry a virgin, or a woman who appears to be virginal. Knowing this, too many young women are reluctant to plan for birth control.

It is not only men who are guilty of anachronistic standards. Often enough, the idea that sexual activity is sinful infects women. There are women who deride or think less of other women who are successfully enjoying sexual relationships. Sometimes this is motivated by envy, but just as often it is the result of a subconscious acceptance of the pervasive patriarchal viewpoint. There are women who desire romance, but who, because of the subconscious effect of their cultural training, would feel a sense of shame if they prepared for a sexual en-

3

counter by planning for contraception. They believe they need to maintain the illusion of sexual spontaneity, of being overcome by passion, and too often have an unwanted pregnancy as a result.

The supreme court decision in Roe vs. Wade has given women some respite, but it has also set in motion an atavistic movement to reverse or subvert that decision and return women to their former legal status. Tears for the souls of unborn babies notwithstanding, this movement is in large measure based on the conviction that if women are allowed to express their sexuality without restriction as men do God will be offended, and that women must therefore be forced to pay for the sin of sexual enjoyment by going through the pain and risks of pregnancy and childbirth.

It would be wonderful if there were a perfect system of birth control so that women could enjoy a complete and secure sexual freedom, and all the children born into the world would be loved and wanted and well cared for, but such is not the case. The question to be answered is: who should decide, when contraceptives fail, whether or not a woman should carry a pregnancy to term? Since only the woman herself knows the details of her circumstances, whether rich or poor, healthy or ill, strong or weak, loved or unloved, cared for or abandoned, only the woman herself has the knowledge necessary to make an informed decision.

Because knowledge is the surest path to freedom, it is hoped that this small volume will show that women have been struggling to break the bonds of their biological nature since time began, and that many of the methods they used in the past might apply to today's world.

PART 1

Witchcraft or Medicine?

For all of recorded history, and probably long before, people have used plants to control their fertility. Women were most likely the first to have discovered that plants had such uses because women are most affected by the rigors of pregnancy, childbirth, and child rearing. There is no doubt that women were responsible for keeping the knowledge of herbal contraceptives and abortifacients alive to be passed down through the generations.

The role of women as discoverers and preparers of medicines is reflected in the modern symbolism of pharmacy. The goddess of pharmacy is Hygeia, the daughter of Asclepius, the Greek physician/god. While Asclepius used his magic serpent-entwined staff, along with incantations and reading omens, to heal the sick, the preparation of medicines was delegated to Hygeia, goddess of healing. Asclepius was expert in casting out demons, but it was Hygeia who was expert in the identification and preparation of healing herbs.

Why not pregnancy?

There are many good reasons why women might want to control whether or not to have a child. There have been many times in history when too many children might place a family or a community at risk of starvation. There are many circumstances where a woman might be too young or frail to have a child safely. In many more times and places a pregnancy might be evidence of a violation of a sexual custom or taboo that would place a woman (and perhaps her lover, but more often not) at risk of severe public censure or death. Then, of course, a woman may make her living — voluntarily or otherwise — selling her sexual favors, in which case she would probably be unwilling to take the time, trouble, and risk of carrying the child of a stranger.

Pregnancy always involves risk. There are over a dozen possible complications that can threaten the life of the mother or child, or more often both. Even with the discovery of antibiotics and modern developments in obstetrics, having children is still one of the greatest dangers women face.

Contraception and Ancient Law

In ancient times, from the time of the Egyptian Pharaohs to the beginning of the Roman Empire, whether a woman chose to prevent conception or to abort an embryo was her own business, as long as she kept the fact to herself. Though there were differences between countries and cultures, in general a woman was not considered pregnant until the fetus had "quickened" (when the movement of the fetus could be felt through the mother's abdomen). This was usually after the first three months (trimester) of the nine month term. There were some, such as the Stoics, who held that life, or the potential for life, began at conception, and who discouraged or outlawed any artificial means to prevent or terminate pregnancy. But, in practice, the general custom held that an embryo was simply a part of the woman's body, under her control, for at least the first few months of the term. This custom is reflected in Mohammed's later statement that after 120 days, an angel comes down from heaven and places a soul in the fetus, making it a child. Until then, a woman was not considered to be pregnant unless she proclaimed herself so.

The laws of that time were sometimes more concerned with the rights of the father than the health of the mother or infant. A woman who was discovered taking a potion to prevent conception or induce a menstrual flow could, in some places, be charged with depriving her husband of an heir. Such charges were probably seldom used since, if a woman is discreet, an early-term abortion is no different from a normal menstrual period.

Midwives' Secrets

The physicians of the time were well aware of the plants that prevented conception or induced menstruation or abortion. The surviving works of Hippocrates, Dioscorides, and Soranus list many of them. But most of the recipes written by physicians are very general, naming the plants but giving no details of harvesting, curing, or even the amounts to use. There could be several reasons for this. The writers could have assumed that other physicians would be familiar with the details of such recipes because the knowledge was so common; they could have been reluctant to transmit these details because of possible abuse (the Hippocratic Oath had a clause prohibiting the use of vaginal suppositories to induce abortion and many physicians, interpreting the clause as a general prohibition, would only terminate pregnancy to save the life of the mother); or, more likely, the physicians were not as familiar with the harvesting, preparation, and applications of these plants as midwives and nurses.

Midwives and nurses attended most births in ancient times. Trained physicians were relatively few, in most instances more expensive, and usually didn't attend to pregnancies unless there were signs of life-threatening trouble. Midwives could therefore be expected to have known more than physicians about childbirth and its

7

complications. They would have known about the herbs that ease childbirth, and that many of those same herbs could both prevent and terminate pregnancy. They surely had to be discreet about the practice of their contraceptive and abortive arts, but they could practice them in relative safety as long as they were careful and caused no harm to the women who purchased their services.

Contraception and Religion

In the West this changed with the beginning of the Middle Ages. As the Roman Empire disintegrated after the 4th century, the Christian Church gradually became the common religion and arbiter of customs for the feuding peoples of Europe and the Mediterranean area. Regarding abortion, however, the early church was divided.

The Old Testament law (Exodus 21:22-23) only punished abortion as murder if the woman died. If there was harm to the woman, the punishment would be a life for a life, an eye for an eye, a tooth for a tooth, etc. If there was no harm, the only punishment for the abortionist was to pay a fine to the husband as determined by judges. It was this law which apparently led to the idea of punishment for a late-term abortion because a formed (quickened) fetus would almost certainly cause harm to the woman when aborted under ancient conditions. During the first few months after conception, an aborted fetus was not considered to be a separate life, but a part of the woman. As such it was considered, like the woman, to be the property of the husband.

Saint Augustine (354-430), bishop of Hippo and one of the founding fathers of the Latin church, agreed with the Old Testament interpretation. He said that when what is aborted is shapeless and unformed, the

8

law of homicide could not apply because such a thing did not yet have a soul.

Saint Basil (330-379), bishop of Caesarea and one of the founding fathers of the Greek church, disagreed. He claimed that a woman who destroys her fetus should pay the penalty of murder, whether the fetus had quickened or not.

It's probable that Christian church leaders were interested in discouraging and outlawing abortion not so much because they were truly concerned about the soul of an unborn fetus, but because they were trying to increase the numbers of their followers. The Pauline injunction that all sex is sinful, that it can only be tolerated if it takes place within marriage and then only for the purpose of procreation, was based on an attempt by St. Paul to increase the numbers of Pauline Christians as much as to differentiate his version of Christianity from that of the numerous Gnostic Christian sects vying for his followers.

The Christian Gnostics had what would be called a very liberal viewpoint regarding sex, allowing any pleasurable form of sexual expression. They considered this life to be full of hardship and tears, though, and they discouraged procreation because they felt that giving birth would be sentencing more and more people to unhappiness. This put them at a disadvantage to the growing numbers of Pauline Christians.

For centuries the early church was involved in an intense competition with not only numerous sects of Gnostics, but also the established Roman and Greek religions, Judaism, and later Manicheism (a Persian religion). When Christianity became the state religion of Rome in the 4th century, the Christian leaders outlawed these competitors and persecuted their members and leaders, but resurgences of these "pagan" religions kept cropping up for ages. The last of them, the Albigensians, were finally destroyed by an extermination crusade and the Inquisition in the 14th century.

Although the majority of the Christian clergy were sincere in their concern for the souls of unborn infants, this concern was rooted in the desire of the early church leaders to secure for themselves a numerical majority. It was the most practical way to insure that their viewpoint would prevail.

Whatever the reasons, the hands of church leaders became more controlling as time went on. For several centuries customs were in flux as political and religious factions struggled for power, but the words of St. Basil against abortion were having an effect. By the time Charles the Great (Charlemagne) was crowned as the Holy Roman Emperor in 800 A.D. the idea that an embryo had a soul at conception was taking firm hold in the church.

The early church tolerated abortion or punished it only lightly. It recognized the difference in motivation between a woman who had an abortion because of poverty, illness, or too many children, and a woman who had an abortion simply to save her figure. The more frivolous the motivation, the greater the required penance.

Gradually, though, the attitude moved to the prohibition of all abortion, no matter what the motivation, and the claim was made that the purposeful ending of pregnancy at any time was murder. Then, attempts to prevent even potential pregnancy were condemned, leading to the eventual prohibition of any form of contraception. By the 12th century, canon law prohibited the use of any potion to inhibit fertility in any way, and those who knew the secrets of herbal contraception and abortion had to go underground.

As centuries passed, church dogma solidified to an extent that might be termed paranoid, and the accusation of Witchcraft was used to suppress artificial birth control, or any unapproved medical techniques. Using plants for their anti-fertility effects, or even revealing a knowledge of such uses of plants, could lead to a charge of heresy, of being in league with Satan, and to burning at the stake. Gradually, the mention of contraceptive or abortifacient activity was dropped from the accepted lists of medicinal plants, and those who knew about such things kept their knowledge very secret.

Midwives and Witchcraft

For centuries the knowledge of birth control was held by a word-of-mouth network of midwives, nurses, mothers, and daughters, quietly passing the knowledge from generation to generation under the ever-present cloud of the suspicion of heresy and witchcraft.

A thirteenth century Spanish physician, Arnold of Villanova, described how an old woman of Salerno used "diabolical practices" to induce a successful delivery. Using three grains of pepper, the old midwife would say an "Our Father" as she gave the pregnant woman each grain to swallow with wine or water. Instead of saying "deliver us from evil", though, she would say "deliver this woman, O Mary, from this difficult labor". She would then say three more "Our Fathers" with other prayers in the woman's right ear, and the woman would deliver at once. Arnold condemned this technique, but he probably didn't know that pepper contains sparteine, an oxytocic substance which causes uterine contractions. Far from being "diabolical", the combination of this drug with the reassurance of prayer would today be considered a very rational way to aid a difficult delivery.

11

A book about French superstitions describes a method used by "sorcerers" to accelerate childbirth. The woman was seated in a chair and caused to breathe the fumes of a decoction of mint, as well as to swallow a dram of the herb Dittany cooked in wine. As this was done the phrase "Sus camp dur" (meaning unknown) was whispered in her ear. Mints such as pennyroyal and corn mint are known uterine stimulants, as is Dittany. From this it is apparent that those who were considered to be sorcerers and witches knew more about psychology and obstetric medicine than their accusers.

The Rise of Science

The charge of witchcraft and sorcery was not used only against midwives, of course, though they were frequent targets. This cloud of superstition hung over all experimental science, and many who were indiscreet about their experiments to push forward the knowledge of the real world ended their lives at the stake. Scientific inquiry moved ahead, though, century by century, despite the protests of dogmatists who felt threatened by any new knowledge. Finally, by the end of the 18th century when the church had lost most of its political influence, science became more important than religion.

This was no real help to those who wanted or needed birth control, though. Centuries of superstition had taken its toll. The art of herbal contraception was no longer punished as witchcraft, but was instead disdained or laughed at as superstitious nonsense. 19th and early 20th century books of remedies didn't mention the birth control uses of plants because the authors regarded stories of such activity as unscientific "old wive's tales", and didn't believe there could be any such uses.

The knowledge continued, though, passed on from generation to generation of women. It remained underground, hidden, not only from prohibitive laws but also from the numbers of jeering or jealous physicians who began to use political influence to suppress competition from herbalists, midwives, and nurses. In the late 19th century there was an epic struggle for legitimacy between allopathic and homeopathic medicine, and the allopaths won. They are today's Medical Doctors, and their associations now have a legal monopoly on medical education and certification.

Modern Medicine

Today, when clinical abortion is legal and manufactured contraceptives are on drugstore shelves, herbal contraception and abortion are either relatively unknown or regarded as reckless or dangerous. Many famous medical journals have reported death or illness from the misuse of these "folk remedies", but few have ever reported or studied the successful use of such remedies, or admitted that over 25% of the medicines doctors use today are derived directly from such remedies.

The studies of herbs that have been done have focused only on analyzing their usefulness to the medical profession, and only in a particular way. They have not tried to find the best plants for a particular purpose, whether contraception or early term abortion, or the best methods of growing, harvesting, and preparing them so that women can make their own educated decisions about whether and how to prepare and use them themselves. Instead, the studies have obtained plants that have been used for fertility control for ages, and have taken them apart to isolate the active substances to understand how they work so that drug companies can manufacture pure, isolated substances for physicians to prescribe.

There is nothing negative about this in itself, of course. The classical approach to science has always been to take things apart to see how they work, discarding the parts that are ineffectual and using the parts that are useful. Because of the allopathic medical monopoly though, research and development, and the money to fund it, has for years tended to be aimed at maintaining a masculine medical elitism, ignoring or deriding any other approaches to medicine and suppressing them by law where possible.

Scientific studies to analyze how plants affect the human body are highly laudable, and those who conduct them are to be encouraged and congratulated, but more work needs to be done on the preparation of natural remedies in order to re-democratize the medical care process. Anyone who has read the warning label on a box of birth control pills, or the release forms for entry to a hospital, knows that modern medicine is not an exact science. While many Medical Doctors may disdain herbal remedies, the dangers involved in using these "folk remedies" that have been used for over three thousand years can surely be no greater than the risks involved with many modern manufactured medicines.

Thus, in many ways the tendency in medicine has been to take control of people's health away from the people themselves and place it in the hands of "experts". In the following pages we will attempt to alter that trend, at least in regard to returning the control of their own reproduction back to women, by providing factual information about some of the plants that have been used through the ages as contraceptives and early-term abortifacients.

PART 2

Introduction to Fertility-Affecting Plants

Substances that control fertility can be divided into two general classes — contraceptives and abortifacients. Contraceptives act to prevent conception or to prevent a conceived embryo from being implanted in the uterus. Abortifacients act to expel an implanted embryo from the uterus.

Another term — emmenagogue — has been used to describe substances that promote menstruation whether or not a fertilized embryo is present. Most women know that their menstrual period can be delayed for many reasons besides pregnancy, such as stress or illness. When delayed menstruation occurs without obvious signs of pregnancy, doctors may sometimes prescribe an emmenagogue to promote a woman's menstrual flow. If the delay was due to pregnancy, though, neither the doctor nor the woman would know the difference. Technically, there is no difference between an emmenagogue and an abortifacient, but "emmenagogue" is a much less politically and psychologically loaded term than anything related to the term "abortion".

Fertility-affecting plants act in many ways. They may affect ovulation or conception through hormonal activity, they may affect the chemistry of the lining of the uterus to prevent implantation, they may cause contractions of the uterus to expel an embryo, or they may have a toxic effect on the embryo, causing it to perish and be flushed away with the menstrual cycle. (It should be mentioned that healthy sexually active women frequently have spontaneous abortions without ever knowing it, expelling fertilized embryos with their normal monthly periods for many often-occurring reasons, such as embryonic defects, physiological malfunctions, diet, medicines, injuries, cosmic radiation, or stress.)

Dioscorides, a famous Roman physician in the 1st century A.D., said that White Willow (*Salix alba L.*) leaves acted as a contraceptive. Then, in 1933 it was found that willow contains estriol, an estrogenic hormone, which would be expected to interfere with conception if taken in the correct dosage and at the proper time in the menstrual cycle.

Illustration from a 6th century B.C. Greek vase. It shows Arkesilas, king of the Greek city-state of Cyrene, supervising the weighing and loading of Silphion, the contraceptive plant that was Cyrene's main export. Greek physicians made frequent reference to "Cyreanic Juice" in their recipes for contraceptives. Now extinct, modern tests of related plants (Giant Fennels) have shown contraceptive effects.

Dioscorides also mentions Barrenwort (*Epimedium Alpinum L.*) as a contraceptive. A closely related plant in the same Genus is reported to be a uterine stimulant, which is probably how it interferes with fertility.

Pennyroyal (Hedeoma pulegiodes L.) has been used for birth control since the ancient Greeks. This plant probably works through its toxic effect. **The oil from the plant is poisonous if taken directly. As little as half a teaspoon of the oil can cause a slow, painful death from kidney and liver failure**.

The *CRC Handbook of Medicinal Herbs* lists twelve plants with estrogenic activity, and thirty-eight that work as abortifacients. One researcher went through ancient books and found references to 161 plants used to control fertility, and that over half of them were listed in modern medical references. We will examine several of these plants that are fairly common in the United States to determine how they have been used by women in the past.

RUE

(Ruta graveolens L.)

Other Names: Garden Rue, German Rue, Herb-of-Grace, Ruda, Country Man's Treacle.

Description: A shrub up to 3 feet tall, with spotted, blue-green leaves 2 to 4 inches long, and greenish-yellow flowers 1/2 inch across with toothed petals. The plant has a distinctive fragrance and a bitter taste.

Harvesting: Harvest the leaves when they mature, or just before flowering, and dry them in the shade. Since the active ingredient is a volatile oil, they should not be subjected to heat before use. Gloves should be worn, since the oil in the plant can cause dermatitis in sensitive persons.

Rue is one of the most ancient and effective contraceptive plants. Pregnant women were constantly warned against eating even small amounts of it because of the danger of miscarriage. Even the smell of it has been said to induce abortions. (This is not too farfetched, since the olfactory nerves have a direct effect on the hypothalamus gland, which controls the endocrine system.) It was usually used in an infusion (tea) to bring on a delayed menstruation, but it was also eaten daily in salads as a contraceptive.

The most explicit recipe available calls for stirring 1 ounce of the leaves into 1 pint of very hot (not boiling) water, and then letting it stand for 8 hours. Drinking this is said to bring on menstruation. It was probably made in a teapot and drunk a cup at a time over several hours. Sugar or honey was probably added.

RUE
Ruta graveolens L.

The contraceptive salad was made with other green plants and herbs, with a teaspoon or so of crushed, dried rue leaves sprinkled over the top. The taste of the rue would be hidden among the other flavors.

QUEEN ANNE'S LACE

(Daucus carota L.)

Other Names: Wild Carrot, Bee's Nest Plant, Bird's Nest.

Description: A branching, fuzzy herb, 1 to 3 feet tall, with a thick, fleshy root. The flowers are small, white or yellow, and grow in clusters at the top of the stem. The fruit containing the seeds are small, oblong, and bristly.

Harvesting: Harvest the seeds in late summer after they mature.

Queen Anne's Lace seeds have been used as a contraceptive for over two thousand years. Recent tests show that they have estrogenic activity and affect the hormone balance in pregnant women, inhibiting implantation. They act as both a contraceptive and an early-stage abortifacient.

Women in the Appalachian Mountains, from Pennsylvania to North Carolina, use them this way: every time they have sexual intercourse, they stir a teaspoonful of the seeds into a glass of water and drink it (seeds and all).

In parts of India, women chew some dry seeds every day to reduce their fertility.

QUEEN ANNE'S LACE
Daucus carota L.

GOLDEN GROUNDSEL

(Senecio aureus L.)

Other Names: Liferoot, Squaw Weed, Golden Ragwort, Ragwort, Butterweed, Golden Rod, Golden Senecio, Groundsel, False Valerian, Wild Valerian.

Description: A perennial with bright yellow flowers in a cluster at the top of the single stem. It has heart-shaped leaves near the bottom, and longish oak-like leaves further up. It can be up to three feet tall.

Harvesting: Harvest the whole plant at full bloom.

Although Groundsel has been used in folk and American Indian medicine for ages, its first official listing as an emmenagogue appears to be in a French guide to natural remedies published in 1939. It is in the same family with Artemisia and Wormwood, which have been recognized as fertility control agents for thousands of years, and tests have shown that the active substance is a uterine stimulant. It is said to be one of the safest and surest emmenagogues.

The recipes for Groundsel call for making a tea from it, but they don't call for specific quantities. It's probable that about a half ounce of the dried and crushed flowers, stems and leaves were steeped in 8 to 12 ounces of very hot water for an hour or so, then drunk in small cupfuls for a day or two until menstruation began.

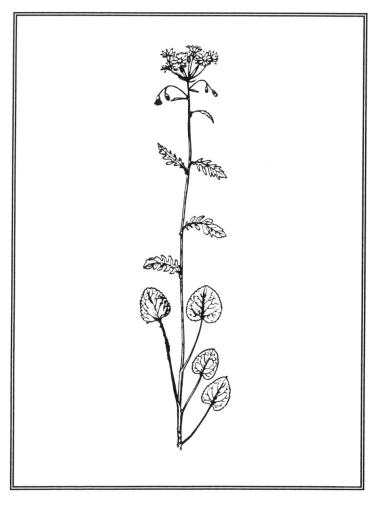

GOLDEN GROUNDSEL
Senecio aureus L.

AMERICAN PENNYROYAL

(Hedeoma pulegoides L.)

Other Names: Mock Pennyroyal, Squaw Mint, Thick-weed, Tickweed, Pudding Grass, Stinking Balm.

Description: 18-inch-high annual, with small hairy oval leaves and tiny aromatic bluish flowers.

Harvesting: Above ground parts in full bloom.

Pennyroyal, like Rue, has been known as a contraceptive and abortifacient since the ancient Greeks. It was mentioned in this context in Aristophanes' play *Peace*, produced in Athens in 421 B.C. According to John Riddle's translation, Quintus Serenus, a 3rd century Roman writer, said that if the woman was less than eight months pregnant and the fetus was weak one should "rush into the bedroom" and administer penny-royal in tepid water. According to Macer's Herbal, written in the 12th century, it should be taken in tepid wine.

Animal experiments with Corn Mint (*Mentha arvensis L.*), a relative of pennyroyal, showed significant results during the post implantation period, 10mg/kg daily from days 7 to 10 resulting in a 90 to 100% loss.

As with most of these herbs, pennyroyal should be taken in a tea. Since fresh leaves contain up to 2% oil, it could be assumed that fresh dry leaves could contain about 50% oil or more by weight. Based on this assumption, and using the above dosage (10mg/Kg) as

AMERICAN PENNYROYAL
Hedeoma pulegioides L.

a guideline, an effective dose for a 100 Lb. woman would seem to be about 1 Gram of crushed leaves steeped in a cup of hot water, drunk every day for several days after pregnancy is suspected. (Remember: 50mg/Kg of oil can be a lethal dose.)

25

TANSY

(Tanacetum vulgare L.)

Other Names: Common Tansy, Double Tansy, Bitter Buttons, Golden Buttons, Parsley Fern, Scented Fern.

Description: A perennial up to three feet tall with fern-like leaves, clusters of small yellow button-like flowers, and a strong, aromatic odor.

Harvesting: Leaves as they mature, flowers at full bloom.

Tansy was first mentioned as an emmenagogue in the medical writings of Saint Hildegard of Bingen, a twelfth century German Benedictine nun. Because this use was apparently unknown to the ancient Greeks, its discovery in the middle ages is a strong indication that, despite the prohibitions imposed by the church, the women who needed them were continuing the search and experimentation for fertility affecting plants.

Tansy oil, like the oil in most fertility affecting plants, is poisonous. As few as ten drops can be fatal. This is why the plant is used in a tea, rather than extracting the oil and using it directly.

When Tansy was used by itself, two or three teaspoons of the crushed dried leaves and flowers would have been steeped in 8 to 12 ounces of hot water for about half an hour, then strained and drunk over a period of several hours. Some sort of sweetener would have been added to lessen the bitter taste.

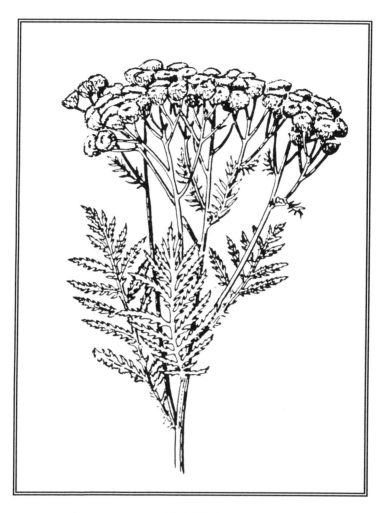

TANSY
Tanacetum vulgare L.

ARTEMISIA
(Artemisia absinthium L.)

Other names: Wormwood, Absinthium, Ajenjo.

Description: Hardy perennial shrubby plant, with small much-indented leaves and yellow hemispherical flower heads at the ends of the branches.

Harvesting: Harvest the leaves when mature.

The plants in the Genus *Artemisia* derive their name from the Greek goddess Artemis, the twin sister of Apollo. As well as her duties as a huntress and guardian of forests and animals, she also protected women in childbirth. It is said that she gave her name to the artemisian herbs because they cure female ills, and can also induce abortion. They have been used as antifertility drugs since ancient times.

The species *absinthium* is the strongest and most bitter of these herbs, and is controversial because it is used to make Absinth, a liqueur which has been banned in most of the world because it causes brain damage. It is still used as an ingredient in Vermouth. The oil has toxic side effects and should be avoided.

Other species, such as *A. vulgaris* (Mugwort) or *A. tridentata* (Sagebrush), are also emmenagogic, but are not as toxic.

A strong tea made from any species of Artemisia can be used to promote menstruation, but if *A. absinthium* is used ancient physicians recommended that it be taken together with Myrrh and Rue.

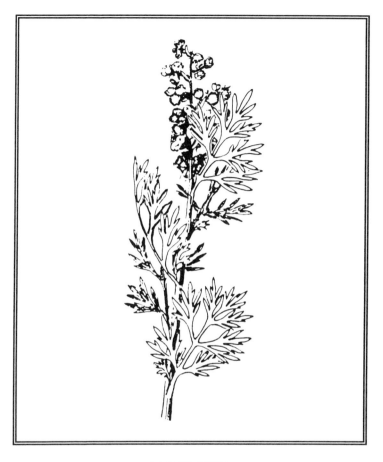

ARTEMISIA
(Artemisia absinthium L.)

These herbs are very bitter. There are frequent references to Wormwood and Gall in the Old Testament, representing punishments for sin or the bitterness of an unfulfilled life.

BLUE COHOSH

Caulophyllum thalictroides L.

Other names: Squaw root, Papoose root, Blueberry root, Blue ginseng, Yellow ginseng.

Description: A perennial up to three feet high, with two- or three-lobed leaflets and yellowish green flowers.

Harvesting: Harvest the roots in Autumn.

Blue Cohosh, as indicated by its most common name — Squawroot, has been used for centuries by Native American women to induce menstrual flow. The Chippewas are said to have used a strong decoction for contraceptive purposes. It is said to be estrogenic and antispasmodic.

Blue Cohosh contains a substance called Caulosaponin, which causes strong uterine contractions. This is why it is also used to hasten childbirth.

The root powder, the most common form sold in herb stores, must be handled with caution because it is very irritating to mucous membranes.

According to J. Parvati, a tea to help regularize the menstrual cycle is made by steeping two tablespoons of Blue Cohosh and two tablespoons of Pennyroyal leaves for thirty minutes per cup of water, then drinking one cup in the afternoon and one cup in the evening for five days before menstruation is due.

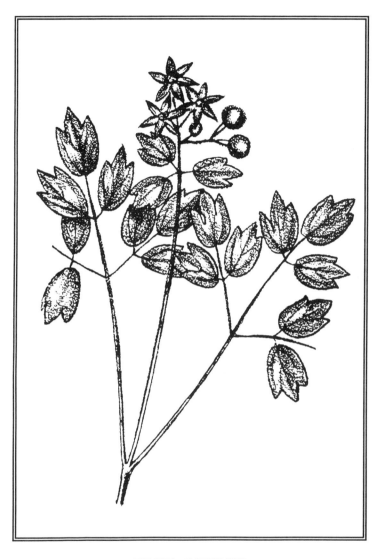

BLUE COHOSH
(Caulophyllum thalictroides L.)

Combination Recipes

Most recipes for promoting a delayed menstrual flow in both ancient and modern literature call for the use of several different herbs. The probable reason for this was that each plant affected a slightly different aspect of the female cycle, and a woman could never be sure of the true cause of a delayed menstruation — stress, illness, medication, or pregnancy. The use of herbs in combination was probably a way of making sure of the desired effect. Also, since each of the herbs had some side effects, the ingredients in some may have counteracted the negative effects of others.

Ancient Recipes

Soranus, the 2nd century gynecologist, gives us this recipe for an early stage abortifacient:

> 3 Drachmas of Rue leaves (.45 oz.), 2 Drachmas of Myrrh (.3 oz.), and 2 Drachmas of Laurel leaves (*Laurus nobilis L.*). Mix them with wine and drink.

We have already discussed Rue. Myrrh comes from the sap of an East African shrub. Besides being one of the gifts of the Magi, it is mentioned frequently in ancient contraceptive recipes. Its name is derived from the legend of Myrrha, daughter of an Assyrian king. Myrrha was ravaged by her father and bore a son — Adonis. The gods helped her escape the continuing advances of her father by changing her into the plant *Commiphora myrrha*, and her tears were used to save girls from the shameful results of incest. Today it is frequently available in spice shops and health food stores. Its effects have not been scientifically tested. Laurel is used in India as an abortifacient, and is listed as an emmenagogue in the *CRC Manual of Medicinal Herbs.*

In the Hippocratic Treatise *Diseases of Women* (4th century B.C.) we find this recipe for an abortifacient:

> A handful of Dittany (*Origanum dictamnus L.*), 2 Drachmas (.3 oz.) of Queen Anne's Lace seeds, Black Cumin (*Nigella sativa L.*). Grind and give as a drink in white wine; after the woman should bathe in warm water.

Dittany has been shown to be an abortifacient, and we have already discussed Queen Anne's Lace. We don't know what Black Cumin does, nor how much to use.

Modern Recipes

A modern herbal recipe for a Female Tea is as follows:

Pennyroyal leaves	4 teaspoons
Tansy leaves & flowers	4 tsp.
Blue Cohosh leaves	3 tsp.
Valerian root	2 tsp.
Rosemary leaves	1 tsp.
Rue leaves	1 tsp.

All ingredients should be dried and crushed. Mix well and divide into 10 doses. Put **one** dose (1 1/2 tsp.) in 2 cups of hot water and steep for half an hour, then strain the tea and drink one third in the morning, one at noon, and one at night. It may be sweetened with honey or sugar. Repeat for up to three days if necessary.

Pennyroyal, Tansy, and Rue have been discussed as emmenagogues. Rosemary (*Rosmarinus officinalis*) is said to relieve cramps and induce menstrual flow, Blue Cohosh (*Caulophyllum thalictroides*, also called Papoose Root) is intended to soothe pains and is emmenagogic, and Valerian (*Valeriana officinalis*) acts as a sedative to quiet nerves and relieve spasms (Valium is a synthetic form of Valerian). If Valerian root is not available, three or four drops of extract per cup will do.

Another tea:

Blue Cohosh	2 tsp.
Cypripedium Root	2 tsp.
Cramp Bark (*Viburnum opulus*)	4 tsp.
Life Root Herb (Groundsel)	3 tsp.
Blue Skullcap(*Scutellaria galariculata*)	2 tsp.
Figwort (*Monotropa uniflora*)	2 tsp.

As above, makes 10 doses. Put 1 1/2 tsp. in 2 cups very hot water and steep for half an hour. Drink 6 Oz. at a time, three times daily. Repeat for up to three days.

Blue Cohosh and Groundsel have been discussed above. Cypripedium Root is said to be a nervous system stimulator. Cramp Bark (also called Black Haw, Highbrush Cranberry and American Sloe) is said to relax spasms and relieve cramps. Blue Skullcap is said to be "quieting". Figwort is said to relieve pain.

Permanent Sterility

It is said that a tea made of the leaves of Solomon's Seal *(Polygonatum multiflora)*, drunk every day for a week will produce permanent sterility. We don't know how it affects the reproductive system, or its side effects.

Hebrew women in Old Testament times who no longer wanted to bear children would drink a "Cup of Roots" to prevent childbearing. In a book on Talmudic medicine the recipe is given as: Alexandrian gum, alum, and turmeric leaves pounded up in grape or plum wine. According to the Talmud, only men were required to "be fruitful and multiply". Women could legally make themselves sterile.

Legal Restrictions

Notice that the ancient recipes are plainly called abortifacients, while the modern are referred to as "teas". This is because there are continuing legal restrictions on information about abortive and emmenagogic herbs. The reasons usually given for these restrictions is that women are not competent to use herbal emmenagogues and abortifacients safely or sanely, and that such things should only be allowed when prescribed by a Medical Doctor.

As well as the prejudice against self-medication, these restrictions also seem to be rooted in the old-fashioned idea that "ignorance is bliss". Much like the idea that keeping teenagers ignorant of sex will reduce the number of teenage pregnancies, many lawmakers seem to think that keeping women ignorant of herbs that can affect fertility will prevent deaths by self-induced abortion. The negative aspect of these restrictions, of course, is that women in desperate situations, and who can't afford (for monetary or social reasons) to solicit medical advice, frequently use methods much more dangerous than herbs to attempt to terminate a pregnancy.

Thousands of women have died from attempts to use soaps, poisons, or foreign objects like coathangers for self-abortion, but there are no records of deaths from herbal remedies except those from overdoses of essential oils, and those deaths were obviously caused by ignorance, not knowledge. Knowledge is power, and the knowledge of herbal birth control should not be restricted to Medical Doctors, but should be available to all women.

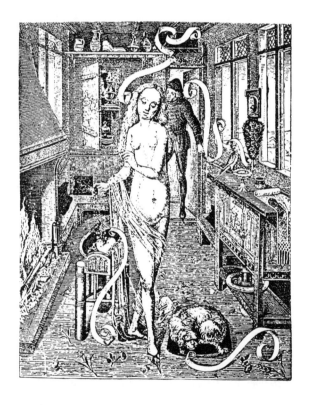

A 16th century illustration of a medieval witch completing a love charm. It is so powerful that as she sprinkles the last of the potion into the fire, her lover is already appearing at the door.

IMPORTANT NOTES

About Essential Oils

The active ingredients in all of these herbal recipes are contained in the oils in the plant. When leaves, flowers, roots or other parts of the plant are used, though, the strength of a particular dose can vary depending on the freshness of the herb, how it was grown, stored, or the time of year — even the time of day — when it was harvested. These variations should not be enough to render the herbs useless, unless the herbs are stored in such a way that the essential oils can dry up or evaporate. Just like spices used for cooking, herbs must be stored in airtight glass containers away from light and changes in temperature.

Because of the difficulty involved in growing or obtaining fresh herbs, some women have made a practice of using the essential oils themselves, which are often available as flavorings in spice shops. **Anyone using essential oils must be very cautious because these oils are highly toxic. An overdose can cause a slow death by liver or kidney failure.**

The reference book *Clinical Toxicology of Commercial Products* lists essential oils as Very Toxic, which means that a dose of 50 milligrams of oil per Kilogram (2.2 Lbs) body weight can be a lethal dose. This works out to a lethal dose of 1 teaspoon for a 150 Lb. person. Oil of Tansy is even more poisonous. The *CRC Handbook* says that ten drops of Tansy oil can be lethal. Savin oil (from the blue berries on the Juniper shrub *Juniperis sabina L.*, which is also used as an abortifacient) can be fatal with a dose of only six drops.

In 1978, according to the *Journal of the American Medical Association*, an 18 year old woman reported to the Denver General Hospital after drinking almost an ounce of pennyroyal oil (equal to 50 gallons of pennyroyal tea). She said she had used Pennyroyal tea many times to induce menstruation, but it was not clear why she drank so much of the oil. She was reported as being very depressed, but it turned out that she wasn't pregnant. The doctors speculated that it had been a suicide attempt. If so she succeeded, dying after seven days.

CAUTION: the use of essential oils is dangerous. Dosages must be measured in drops, not spoonfuls, and an effective dose is very close to a lethal dose. The use of combinations of herbs is safer, and has been tested by millions of women over thousands of years. Many women have died from experimenting to gain this knowledge. For the sake of their memory, no one should ignore it.

About Plant Identification

We have included the botanical Latin names of all the plants we have mentioned to aid in identifying them, as well as including the best pictures available of the primary plants.

Most of these medicinal plants are regarded as weeds, and can be found in vacant lots, by roadsides, and at the edges of fields. Groundsel likes wet or swampy ground. There are other books about herbs with pictures that can help in identification, but the surest way is to consult someone who knows about botany, such as a teacher, nursery owner, garden club enthusiast, city park gardener, herbalist, or the local County Agricultural Extension Service agent.

Another way to obtain these herbs, for those interested in investigating the subject further, is to purchase them from health food stores. Because of their potential misuse, some of them are not allowed to be sent through the mail, but often the seeds are available through catalogs so that they can be grown at home.

Anyone interested in investigating these remedies should read more than just this booklet, which is intended only as an introduction to the subject. Several very informative books are mentioned in the reference section. They are available through bookstores or directly through their publishers, and should also be at most libraries (or available through interlibrary loan).

About Effectiveness

Because there have been virtually no scientific studies of the effectiveness of herbal remedies, we can't predict whether or not they will work 100% of the time, or even which ones will be the most effective for a particular purpose. The only thing we can say with confidence is that these herbs have been continuously used as contraceptives, emmenagogues and abortifacients for thousands of years, which wouldn't be true if they weren't effective at least most of the time. In those cases where the active ingredients have been studied, it has been found that they have the properties necessary to work.

It is important to remember that prompt action is necessary to avoid pregnancy. If a woman suspects that a delayed menstruation is due to pregnancy, and she doesn't want to carry it to term, these herbs are said to be most effective when the embryo is very tiny, in the first two to four weeks. **After the first month, they become more dangerous. After the first trimester, these remedies should not even be considered.**

If a woman is sexually active and concerned about pregnancy, and if she is late in having her period, it would probably be wise for her to use one of the over-the-counter pregnancy tests to check her condition before using one of the herbal emmenagogue recipes. These herbs can be very bitter, and they may upset the digestion and may cause an ill feeling for a few days. For some sensitive persons, they may cause severe nausea and other unpleasant symptoms. They should not be taken without good reason. (Then again, for personal and psychological reasons, some women may not want to confirm a pregnant condition, and may want to use an herbal emmenagogue to start a late period without knowing one way or the other. Contrary to what many may say, women are very sensitive to abortion, and take reproductive matters very seriously.)

Herbal remedies should not be taken just because they're somehow more "natural" than manufactured remedies. They should only be used when they can cure something that a manufactured remedy cannot cure, or by those who simply can't afford the cost of the manufactured remedy, or perhaps the doctor's prescription that might be required to get it. The virtues of manufactured remedies are that they have been tested extensively, and whatever negative side effects they have are known (at least by good doctors). When they are taken under a doctor's guidance they are probably safer than herbal remedies, which have only been tested through experience.

This is especially true of contraceptives. No one can say whether Queen Anne's Lace seeds are safer or more effective than birth control pills, diaphragms used with a spermicidal foam, or other methods of contraception. What can be said is that the seeds have not been scientifically tested, and that it's possible to sue the manufacturer of the other remedies if something goes wrong with them.

The only real virtue of herbal emmenagogues is that they fill a need which has not yet been filled by the medical community. Herbal emmenagogues can serve as a "morning after pill", preventing or ending a pregnancy in its first stages. They can be tried when contraceptives fail to work, and before it becomes necessary to hire the services of an abortion clinic. This may be appealing to many women, since it appears that abortion clinics will continue to be targeted by radical groups for some time, making what is already an unpleasant experience into a threatening or possibly dangerous journey.

RU 486, the new "morning after pill" which is essentially an emmenagogue and accomplishes the same thing, is available in Europe by prescription, but it will probably not be available in this country for quite awhile. The politics of reproduction is still a highly charged issue, and dogmatists are still trying to keep women from having control of their own lives, just as they did in the Middle Ages. Those opposed to it will try to prevent the importation of RU 486 for as long as possible.

How RU 486 works

RU 486 (the RU stands for Roussel-Uclaf, the French pharmaceutical company) blocks the activity of progesterone, a steroid hormone that's necessary for the body to maintain a pregnancy.

During the first two weeks of a woman's menstrual cycle, estrogen and other hormones promote the growth of an ovarian follicle (which contains the egg) and the cells lining the uterus. When the egg is released, the remaining part of the follicle becomes a tiny gland, called the corpus luteum, which secretes a continuous stream of progesterone. This progesterone prepares the lining of the uterus to accept and nourish an embryo, relaxes the uterine muscles to prevent contractions, and firms the cervix, inhibiting dilation.

41

If the egg is not fertilized, the corpus luteum degenerates after about 12 days, and the resulting decline in progesterone causes the lining of the uterus to shed its nourishing layers, resulting in the menstrual flow. This decline in progesterone also allows the cervix to soften and dilate, and stops the relaxation of the uterine muscles, often resulting in the menstrual cramps with which all women are familiar.

If the egg is fertilized, it will implant itself in the uterine lining on about the sixth day. The portion of the conceptus that will develop into the placenta secretes a hormone called human chorionic gonadotropin (HCG), which signals the corpus luteum to continue to secrete progesterone until about the eighth week, when the placenta is fully developed and takes over the secretion of hormones.

RU 486 is a chemical that looks to the body like progesterone, but doesn't do the things that progesterone does. When it is given after implantation, it is absorbed by the uterine lining which thinks it's getting real progesterone, but, because RU 486 doesn't operate in the same way, the lining begins to break down, the embryo is detached from the uterine wall, the placenta stops secreting HCG which stops the corpus luteum from secreting progesterone, the lining breaks down further, and a menstrual flow develops.

Because RU 486 alone doesn't cause the strong uterine contractions necessary to expel an embryo completely, after several days a dose of prostaglandin is given to induce contractions and insure a complete expulsion of the embryo and uterine lining.

Birth Control Pills

Birth control pills work differently than RU 486. They don't imitate a hormone. Instead, they use synthetic hormones to fool the body into thinking things are normal, then, by withdrawing those hormones at the right time a normal menstrual period is produced, but without an egg.

The estrogen necessary to develop an egg is produced by the ovaries, but the ovaries (and other glands) are controlled by the pituitary gland, a kind of master controller. The pituitary monitors the amount of hormones in the blood, and whenever it decides there should be more hormones, it secretes a signal hormone, a tropin, to prompt the right gland to produce more hormones. If it detects a shortage of estrogen, it releases an estrogen tropin and the ovaries produce more estrogen. It takes a lot of estrogen to develop an egg.

Birth control pills are made of estrogen and progesterone, not enough to cause an egg to develop, but just enough to fool the pituitary gland so that it doesn't release estrogen tropin. Developing eggs require a lot of hormones, so this actually prevents ovulation. The pills are taken for the first twenty days of the cycle, and the smaller amount of hormone produces only a slight thickening of the uterine lining. When they're stopped this lining sloughs off, much like a regular menstrual flow. (Some pill packages have placebos or sugar pills for the last week of the cycle so the woman doesn't get out of the habit of taking them.) If by chance an egg develops, even if it's fertilized, there aren't enough hormones present to prepare the uterus for implantation.

Women and Reproduction

Women have always carried the primary responsibilities for human reproduction. It is a role that has been thrust on them throughout history not only by their biological makeup, but by intense cultural conditioning.

The arguments over whether this conditioning is positive or negative, or whether it's propagated more by patriarchal men, women contented with the role, or accidents of history are beyond the scope of this volume. What is clear is that women frequently have had little choice about the matter.

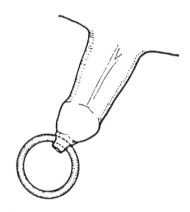

Male infibulation, equivalent to a female chastity belt, was a contraceptive technique sometimes used in Roman times. It prevented conception by preventing copulation. Today, when it's difficult to convince a man to wear a condom, it probably wouldn't be very popular.

After 4,000 years of recorded history it is only in the last few decades that women have had a small taste of the sort of sexual and occupational freedom that men seem to have always enjoyed. Because choice is what freedom is all about, if women want more freedom they must continue to insist on the right to sexual freedom, as well as to choose whether or not they want to assume the responsibilities of motherhood.

The popular arguments against abortion, like the arguments against birth control decades ago, center on the rights of the unborn embryo, not the rights of the woman. But no one brings these arguments to their logical and tyrannical conclusion: if embryos have rights that should be protected by law, then the law must test every fertile woman every month to see whether or not she is pregnant, and must then regulate the medical and dietary habits of every pregnant woman. If those who oppose a woman's choice to end a pregnancy had their way, every woman would wear a monitoring bracelet from menarche to menopause, would be forced to obey strict dietary and medical regulations, and would be quite literally a slave to her biological makeup.

The truth is that an embryo, as long as it resides in and gains nourishment from the woman in whose body it was conceived, is a part of the woman's body. As such, it is her property to accept or reject according to her will, and her will alone. Until this is recognized by both the law and the culture, women will not be truly free.

It is to promote this freedom of choice that this volume has been written. Hopefully in the future it will be possible for individual women to make these choices for themselves, privately, based on their own individual desires. Perhaps information about herbal emmenagogues will become widespread, and women will become more knowledgeable about their reproductive systems and about the best herbs to use. Perhaps a benevolent foundation will sponsor scientific studies of these herbs for that purpose. When that happens politics will cease to matter. Women will be able to control their own fertility with herbs from their own backyard gardens.

AFTERWORD

We would like to encourage any readers who have had actual experiences with using herbs for birth control purposes, whether positive or negative, to tell us about them. Though the information will be anecdotal rather than scientific, it may be useful to other women. We are already contemplating a revised and expanded edition of this work, and, because of the lack of scientific data, we would like to include the real-life stories of experienced women. Complete privacy will be respected in all cases.

Send any such letters to:

Cloud Chief Publishing
HBC Project
PO Box 1664
Weatherford, OK 73096

REFERENCES

None of the information contained in this booklet is original, nor is it meant to be. Because this is not an academic work, it has not been footnoted, but readers are encouraged to consult the following references for further information.

Contraception and Abortion from the Ancient World to the Renaissance by John M. Riddle. 1992. Boston: Harvard University Press.
(Buy this book. It is the best book available on the use of herbs for birth control throughout history. Order it from your local bookstore or direct from the publisher.)

Hygieia - A Woman's Herbal by J. Parvati. 1978. Berkeley: Bookpeople. (Very New Age. Sympathetic Magic, Astrology, and Herbs in a gently feminist manner. Highly recommended. Order through the Tattered Cover bookstore - 800-833-9327, or your local bookstore.)

CRC Handbook of Medicinal Herbs by James A. Duke. 1985. Boca Raton, FL: CRC Press. (An excellent work by the former Chief of the Medicinal Plant Resources Laboratory of the USDA. Discusses the herbal uses and toxicity of 365 commonly sold herbs, with an extensive bibliography.)

Plants Used by Primitive Peoples to Affect Fertility by Henry de Laszlo and Paul S. Henshaw. 1954. *Science* 119:626-631. (Informative Science journal article.)

Oral Contraceptives in Ancient and Medieval Times by John M. Riddle and J. Worth Estes. *American Scientist*, May-June 1992 Pp. 226-233. (Very informative article. Prelude to Riddle's book listed above. Available from Sigma Xi, The Scientific Research Society, Tel. # 919-549-0097.)

Pennyroyal Oil Poisoning and Hepatotoxicity by John B. Sullivan, et al. *Journal of the American Medical Association*, Dec. 28, 1979. Vol. 242, No. 26, Pp. 2873-74. (Medical details of two cases of Pennyroyal oil poisoning.)

The People's Herbal - A Family Guide to Herbal Home Remedies by Dr. M.A. Weiner. 1984. NY: Putnam. (General herbal remedies)

Clinical Toxicology of Commercial Products by Gosselin, Smith, and Hodge. 5th Edition. 1985. Baltimore: Williams & Wilkins. (Manual for doctors on poisonous substances. Discusses toxicity of Essential Oils.)

Health Plants of the World by F. Bianchini & F. Corbetta. 1977. New York: Newsweek Books. (Many color illustrations.)

Contraception Through the Ages by B.E. Finch and Hugh Green. 1963. Springfield, IL: Charles C. Thomas. (Discusses many of the methods used through history, including listing some plants. Also talks about history of struggle to legalize contraception.)

Using Plants for Healing by Nelson Coon. 1963. Hearthside Press. (Good chapter on the preparation of herbs, including collecting, drying, and storing.)

Strictly Female - An Evaluation of Brand-Name Health & Hygiene Products for Women by Carol Ann Rinzler. 1981. NY: New American Library. (Good general reference for women, one table discussing herbs and possible allergic reactions.)

Medical Botany - Plants affecting Man's Health by W.H. Lewis & M.P.F. Elvin-Lewis. 1977. NY: John Wiley & Sons. (Section on reproductive system discusses fertility-affecting plants.)

A Guide to the Medicinal Plants of the United States by Arnold & Connie Krochmal. 1973. NY: Quadrangle/NY Times Book Co. (An excellent field guide with many illustrations.)

The Midwife and the Witch by T.R. Forbes. 1966. New Haven: Yale University Press. (Concentrates on superstitions regarding sex and childbirth. Some history of midwifery in the Middle Ages, generally critical.)

The Divine Origin of the Craft of the Herbalist by Sir E.A. Wallis Budge. 1928. London: Culpeper House. (History of ancient Herbals.)

Pictorial History of Ancient Pharmacy by Hermann Peters. 1899. Chicago: G.P. Engelhard & Co. (Interesting history of pharmacy with chapters on ancient aphrodisiacs and alchemy.)

Septic Abortion by R.H. Schwarz, M.D. 1968. Philadelphia: J.P. Lippincott. (Grim and sobering technical manual about abortion gone wrong. Written before Roe v. Wade, it discusses facts and risks of criminal abortion.)

Sex in History by Reay Tannahill. 1982. Briarcliff Manor, NY: Scarborough House. (Excellent book describing sexual mores and practices through history. Highly recommended.)

Health and Healing a newsletter edited by Dr. Julian Whitaker, M.D. March 1993 issue. (An excellent newsletter dedicated to a non-toxic approach to medicine. Frequently discusses natural remedies. Available by calling 301-424-3700.)

Sources

Here is a list of a few sources for herbs, seeds, and information on herbal remedies. For those who are serious about investigating fertility-affecting plants, it might be wise to order seeds, since if this information becomes widespread those who oppose abortion, as well as those who oppose homeopathic remedies, may work to have the sale of these herbs made illegal. In some cases, such as that of Tansy, it is already illegal to send them through the mail.

Aphrodisia
282 Bleeker St. N.Y., N.Y. 10014
212-989-6440

Bee Creek Botanicals (Wholesalers)
Austin, TX   78725
512-331-4244

Smile Herb Shop
4908 Berwyn Rd. College Park, MD 20740
301-474-8791

Health Center for Better Living
6189 Taylor Rd., Naples, FL 33942
813-566-2611
Herbs, herb seeds, and books on herbal remedies.

Southern Exposure Seed Exchange
PO Box 158, North Garden, VA 22959
Herb, flower and vegetable seeds, books and information about gardening and saving seeds.

The Redwood City Seed Company
PO Box 361
Redwood City, CA   94064
Catalog $1

APPENDIX

MODERN CONTRACEPTIVES

The following is a list of commonly used contraceptives, their relative effectiveness, advantages, disadvantages, and possible risks. (Moderately effective means: Don't be surprised if it doesn't work.)

Calendar Rhythm   Moderately effective

This method requires no equipment or chemicals, but it requires intelligence, motivation, and the discipline to sustain periods of abstinence. It also requires that the woman have a regular, predictable cycle.

Temperature Rhythm   Moderately effective

No equipment or chemicals, but also requires discipline and high motivation, and fevers can affect the temperature readings, throwing off the cycle. (Remember the old joke: What do you call people who use the rhythm method?   Parents!)

Intercourse While Breastfeeding Unpredictable

This method requires no equipment or chemicals, but ovulation can begin anytime after pregnancy, particularly after the first two or three months.

Coitus Interruptus   Moderately effective

This method has the advantage of requiring no equipment or chemicals. The disadvantage, of course, is that the woman must depend on the man to interrupt the sexual act at the peak of his own excitement and

51

ejaculate outside of her. There is also the possibility that some sperm may be present in the man's preseminal lubricating fluid.

Douching   Not very effective

This method not only requires equipment, but it requires the woman to interrupt the quiet moments after a passionate embrace to manipulate rubber bags and hoses. It is also not very good at eliminating sperm from the vagina and cervix. Sperm move quickly. Frequent douching can also promote various vaginal infections by washing out the body's natural fluids.

Spermicides   Moderately effective

Spermicides don't require a doctor's prescription, but they can be messy and taking time out to insert them can break up a romantic moment. Some women may also be allergic to some of them.

Condom   Very effective

Condoms don't require a prescription, but men sometimes complain about using them. There is some loss of sensation for the man, and some interruption of the passionate moments for installation (which can sometimes result in the loss of the man's erection unless creative or playful methods are used). We regret to say it, but they also sometimes break or slip off.

Diaphragm with spermicide   Very effective

Diaphragms are relatively inexpensive, but they must be fitted by a doctor and the woman must be trained to insert one properly, using plenty of spermicide. They can be inserted hours before a sexual encounter and if properly fitted they will not be noticed by the woman using it. It is possible, though, for the diaphragm to be

pushed away from the cervix during some encounters,
depending on the depth of the vagina, the size of the
penis, and the type and level of activity during intercourse. Also, some women may have allergic reactions
to some spermicides.

IUD   Very effective

With an IUD there is no interruption of romance, and
if properly fitted they should not be noticed by the
woman. They must be fitted by a doctor, though, and
there are sometimes medical complications from their
use, such as perforations of the uterus, cramps, uterine
inflammations, and bleeding.

The Pill   Most effective

There are many types of birth control pills, but all of
them have synthetic estrogen or progesterone or a
combination of the two. They are almost foolproof if
taken regularly, but they must be prescribed by a doctor
and the woman must be careful to get regular medical
checkups because, though only a small percentage of
women have negative side effects, the side effects can
be serious. Some women must try four or five different
types before finding one that works well. The risks, for
those women susceptible to them, are thromboembolisms
(blood clots forming in veins, then breaking loose and
damaging vital organs), liver changes or damage, changes in metabolism, depression, and an increased risk of
cancer in women with a family history of breast cancer.

Note: There are three kinds of estrogen: estrone
and estradiol (both synthetics), and estriol, a plant-
derived estrogen identical to that in a woman's body. It
has been known for twenty years that estrone and
estradiol are carcinogenic, while estriol has been shown
to inhibit cancers. It has also been shown that synthetic
progesterones, if not dangerous, are not as helpful to the

body as natural, plant-derived progesterone, particularly regarding bone loss in menopausal women. Birth control pills and hormone replacement treatments for women are almost exclusively made up of synthetic hormones, and therefore should be used with caution and only under the care of a good doctor who understands the risks and takes care to monitor patients closely.

The problem is not primarily with the drug companies who manufacture the chemicals, though they should share a good portion of blame for the way things are set up, but with the FDA and the legal system we use for approving the sale of medicines. Our laws give the Food and Drug Administration enormous power to regulate not only medicines, but even information about substances that could be used as medicines. The FDA must approve any substance sold on a therapeutic basis, and can prosecute violations in its own courts, with no juries, and its decisions are not subject to challenge in court.

With a very expensive approval process, it is often not worth the money for any company to try and get a relatively inexpensive plant-derived product onto the market. It is more cost-effective to synthesize a substance, which makes it patentable, and deliver that substance to the market with an exclusive right to manufacture and sell it.

Drug companies are neither totally innocent or totally evil. It is the legal system that is flawed.

Anyone interested in changing this situation should contact their U.S. Senator about the Health Freedom Act of 1992, introduced by Sen. Hatch.

Anyone interested in safer hormone therapy should subscribe to the *Women's Health Connection*, 1-800-366-6632 for information about Phytoestrogens.